Microsoft

PowerPoint

CW00446821

explained

Other Titles of Interest

Microsoft

PowerPoint

2000

explained

David Weale

Bernard Babani (Publishing) Ltd
The Grampians
Shepherds Bush Road
London W6 7NF
England

Please Note

Although every care has been taken with the production of this book to ensure that any instructions or any of the other contents operate in a correct and safe manner, the Author and the Publishers do not accept any responsibility for any failure, damage or loss caused by following the said contents. The Author and Publisher do not take any responsibility for errors or omissions.

The Author and Publisher make no warranty or representation, either express or implied, with respect to the contents of this book, its quality, merchantability or fitness for a particular purpose.

The Author and Publisher will not be liable to the purchaser or to any other person or legal entity with respect to any liability, loss or damage (whether direct, indirect, special, incidental or consequential) caused or alleged to be caused directly or indirectly by this book.

The book is sold as is, without any warranty of any kind, either expressed or implied, respecting the contents, including but not limited to implied warranties regarding the book's quality, performance, correctness or fitness for any particular purpose.

No part of this book may be reproduced or copied by any means whatever without written permission of the publisher.

© 1999 BERNARD BABANI (publishing) LTD

First Published - October 1999

British Library Cataloguing in Publication Data

A catalogue record for this book is available from the British Library

ISBN 0 85934 476 2

Cover Design by Gregor Arthur

Cover Illustration by Adam Willis

Printed and bound in Great Britain by Bath Press

Preface

Welcome, I wrote this book to help you in learning how to use the program in a practical way. It is intended to explain the program in a way that I hope you will find useful, and that you will learn by doing.

Each section of the book covers a different aspect of the program and contains various hints and tips which I have found useful and may enhance your work.

The text is written both for the new user and for the more experienced person who wants an easy to follow reference.

You should know how to use the basic techniques of Microsoft® Windows® 95/98; if you do not, there are many excellent texts on the subject.

I hope you learn from this book and have fun doing so.

David Weale, October 1999

Trademarks

About the author

David Weale is a Fellow of the Institute of Chartered Accountants and has worked in both private and public practice. At present, he is a lecturer in business computing.

Contents

The Pull Down Menus... 91

Beginnings

When you load Microsoft® PowerPoint for the first time, you will see the screen shown below.

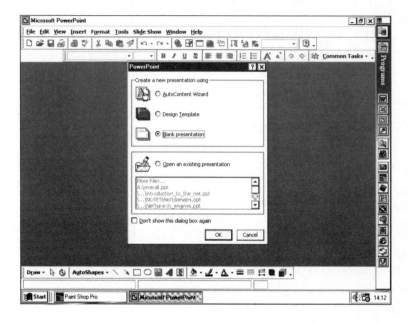

The Pull Down Menus

File   Edit   View   Insert   Format   Tools   Slide Show   Window   Help

Along the top of the screen are the pull down menus.

When you click the (left) mouse button on any of these, a pull down menu will appear.

Each contains several related commands (some of which can also be carried out using the toolbar buttons). These pull down menus are dealt with later in the book.

The Toolbars

There are two toolbars; these contain buttons, which you click to carry out activities or commands.

The toolbar buttons are an alternative to using the pull down menus and you can add or remove buttons as you wish (to reflect your own requirements - **Tools, Customise**).

One of the most useful buttons is **Common Tasks**, which contains the following commands (click then arrow to the right of the words to pull down the list).

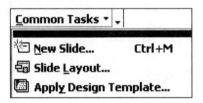

If you position the mouse pointer over any of the toolbar buttons, a description will appear.

If you click the right-hand mouse button while pointing at any button a pull down menu will appear with various commands (depending upon the button chosen).

Your First Presentation

There are four choices:

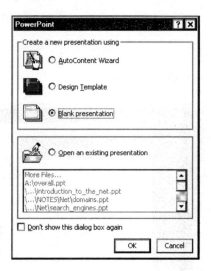

❖   AutoContent wizard

❖   Design Template

❖   Blank presentation

❖   Open an existing presentation

These choices are also available by pulling down the **File** menu and selecting **New** or by clicking the **New** button. We will look at each in turn.

AutoContent Wizard

This guides you through a series of steps. You enter various details or make choices in each. The result is a professional presentation that you can create in a very short time.

The first screen is shown below.

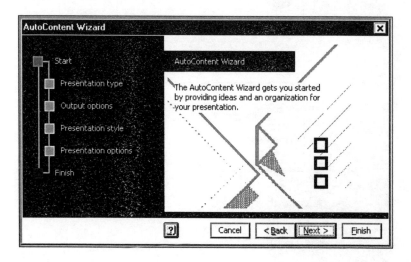

This is followed by a series of other screens, the content of which will differ depending upon your choices at each stage.

As you can see from the next screen, there are a variety of different presentation wizards to choose (including web page presentations that can be put onto the Internet or your organisation's Intranet).

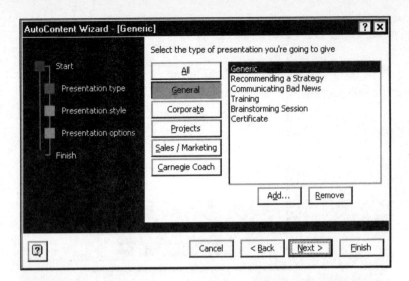

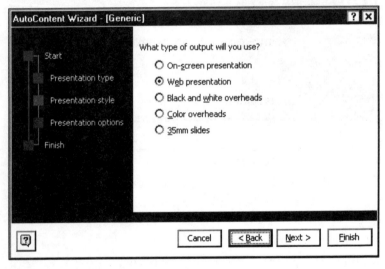

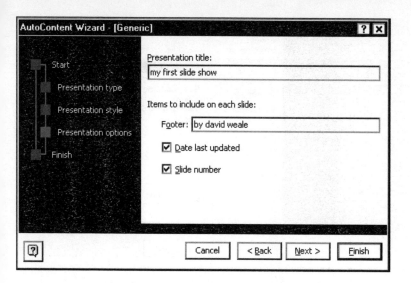

When you have finished, the Wizard leaves you with an Outline of the presentation with prompting text already in place.

All you have to do is to alter the text (by highlighting and overwriting) to whatever you want to say.

You can add or delete slides as you wish.

An example of the finished layout is shown below.

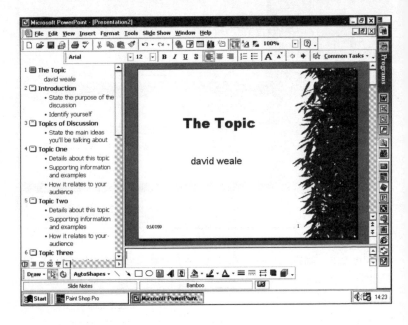

Templates

The second option is the template. After selecting this, you will see the following.

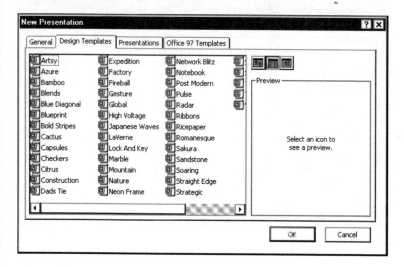

You can look at the display in three different ways as **Large Icons**, **List** or **Details**. To alter the display, click on the appropriate button (to the right of the dialog box).

A small preview of your selected design is shown on the right.

After you have chosen your design and clicked on the **OK** button, you will be asked to select a **Layout**. The default is the title layout.

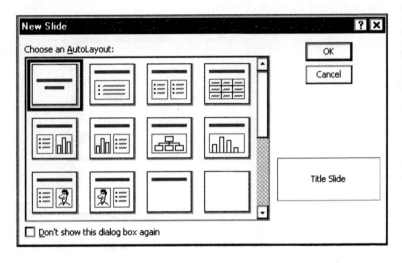

Finally you will see the slide; you then add your own text by clicking and typing in the appropriate place.

Blank Presentation

The third option is the blank presentation. This gives you a choice of layout without the addition of a design. The only dialog box is shown below.

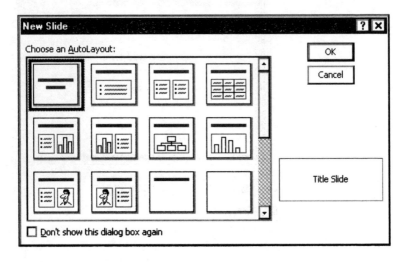

This is an ideal choice if you wish to apply a design at a later stage.

A blank presentation looks like this.

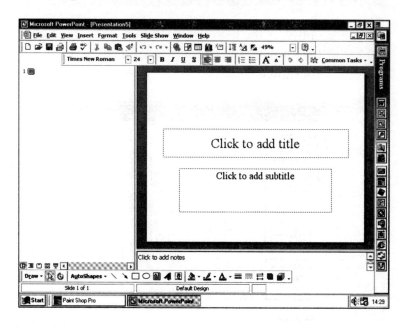

Existing presentations

Selecting this option displays the **Open** dialog box. You need to find the file you wish to open.

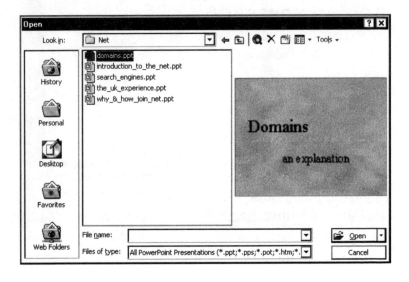

Common Tasks

Adding new slide

You use this to add a new slide after the current slide.

Altering the layout

To alter the layout, click on the **Common Tasks** button, followed by the **Slide Layout** button (upper toolbar) and select an alternative layout. This is slightly different to the original layout screen as it allows you to **Reapply** a layout to an existing slide.

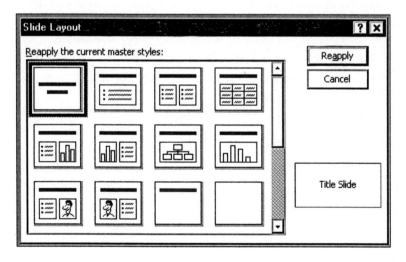

Altering the Design

You can click on **Apply Design Template** (**Common Tasks** button) to alter the design. This lets you alter a design at any time.

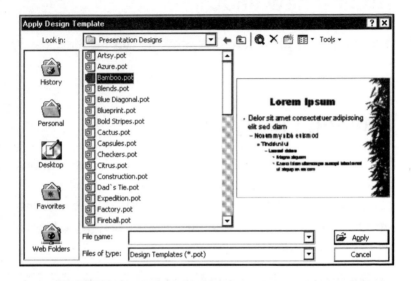

Be careful to apply the design early on, if you alter the fonts or layout of a slide show and **then** alter the design, the new design may impose its own formatting on the slides, e.g. fonts and colour scheme.

Looking at Your Slides

There are several ways of looking at the slides. You can use the **View** menu or the buttons along the bottom left of the screen.

❖   Normal

❖   Outline

❖   Slide

❖   Slide Sorter

❖   Slide Show

Normal View

This is the way the slides are normally displayed.

Unlike previous versions of the program, this also displays
the outline on the left and the notes pane along the bottom
of the screen.

You can make changes to the slides by altering the text in
the outline or in the slide itself.

Both the outline pane and the notes pane can be made
larger or smaller by clicking on the divide and dragging the
pane.

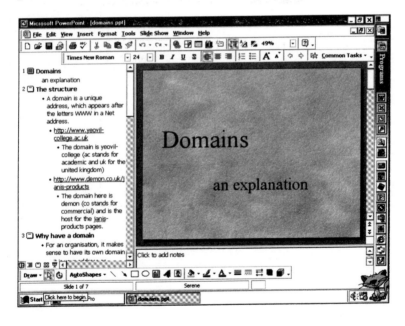

You can move from slide to slide by using the buttons on the right of the screen.

Zooming

To size the display, either click the **Zoom Control** button on the upper toolbar, or pull down the **View** menu and choose **Zoom**. This gives more control as you can enter a figure in the **Percent** box.

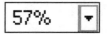

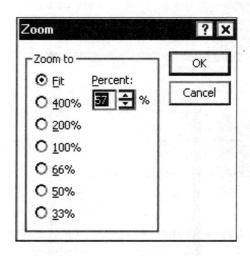

Outline View

The titles and main text of all your slides are shown, each slide is numbered and they are shown in sequence.

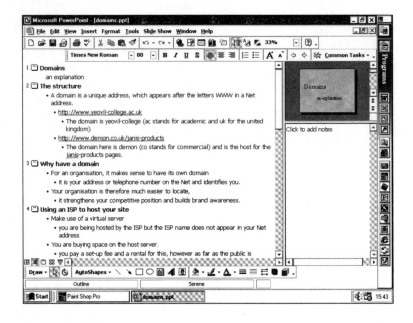

Being able to see all the main text in this way lets you alter the content and rearrange it more easily.

You can also add/alter text, graphics and multimedia effects using the slide pane (top right-hand corner of the window).

In addition there is a notes pane on the right where you can add notes to your slides (these can be printed out if you wish).

Importing outlines

You can import outlines from other programs, such as Word and from web (HTML files) as well as more traditional file types.

The outline buttons are described here (you need to pull down the **View** menu, followed by **Toolbars** and then **Outlining**).

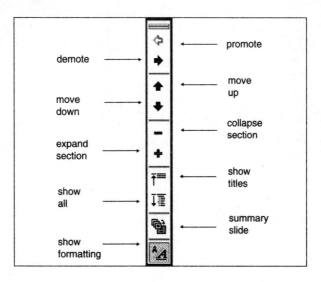

You can use the **Tab** key to demote a line or use **Shift** and **Tab** to promote a line (instead of the buttons).

Slide View

This displays the slides full screen, so that you can add to or alter them.

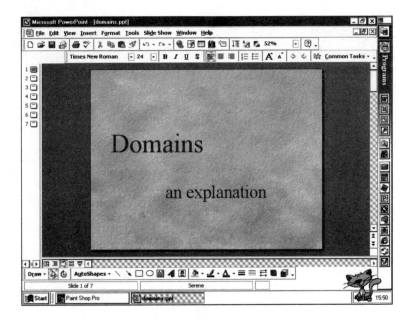

Slide Sorter View

You can look at all the slides by clicking on the **Slide Sorter View** button (along the bottom of the screen).

You will see the following display.

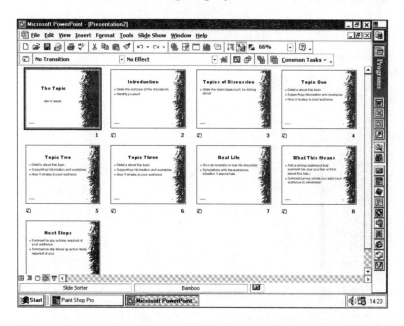

This displays (small) images of all your slides and you can rearrange the sequence or add/delete slides, etc.

To alter the size of the slides use the **Zoom** button.

To move the slides around, simply click on a slide with the mouse and then drag it to a new position (between two slides). The other slides will rearrange themselves.

You can **Select All** from the **Edit** menu and apply special effects such as **Transitions** and **Animations** to all the slides if you are in **Slide Sorter View**.

Slide Show

You can view the slide show as it would appear (projected onto a screen) by clicking on the **Show** button along the bottom of the screen.

Domains

an explanation

Using a projector is the most effective way of presenting and you can build in special effects such as **Transitions** and **Animations** (which you cannot do if you print the slides onto OHP film).

The Slide Show menu

If you click the **right-hand** mouse button during a slide show, the following menu is displayed.

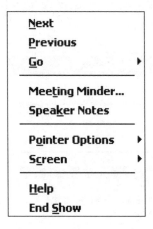

The most important of these are explained below.

Next/Previous/Go

Use these commands to move to the next or previous point (not slide).

The **Go** option has a sub menu.

Slide Navigator/By Title

Selecting one of these displays a list of slides (Navigator) or titles (Title), if you choose one of these then the corresponding slide will be displayed. The Navigator menu is shown for reference.

Custom Show

This jumps to a custom show (you have to have created a custom show - **Slide Show** and **Custom Shows**).

Meeting Minder

You can add notes or minutes during the presentation by selecting this option. Participants in an online meeting will all be able to see the notes.

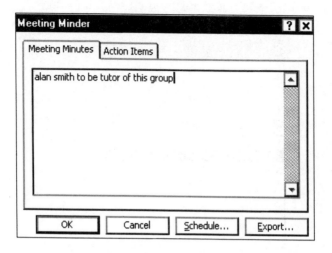

If you have **Word** or **Outlook** installed you can **Export** or **Schedule** the text.

Speaker Notes

If you have created speaker notes, these can be displayed on your screen.

You can also add notes during the presentation.

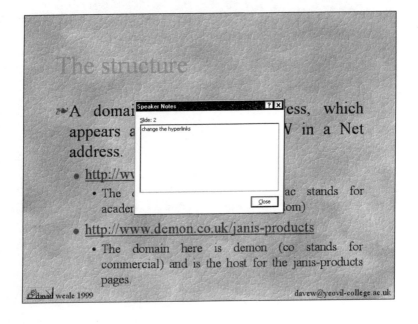

Pointer Options

You can change the arrow to a pen so that you can write on the screen (whether this is legible depends upon your mouse control).

You can hide the pointer so that it never appears and you can alter the colour of the pen.

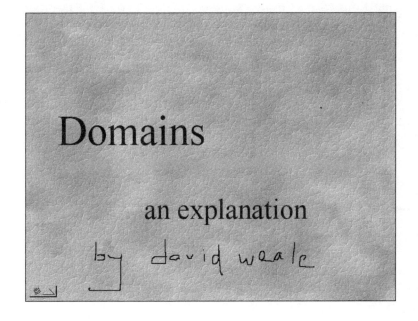

Screen/End Show

You can **Pause** the screen (when using automatic timings), **Black** the screen and if you have used the pen, you can **Erase** the pen (your writing).

Pau<u>s</u>e
<u>B</u>lack Screen
<u>E</u>rase Pen

I suggest you end the slide show either with a black screen or have a final slide that you can leave while you answer questions, for example your company logo. This is more professional than just ending the show.

You can also choose to **End Show**, which ends it abruptly.

Setting up a self-running slide show

Often it is useful to set up a slide show that is self-running e.g. at an exhibition.

You do this in two stages, firstly setting up the show and secondly deciding upon the timings either manually or automatically (how long each slide will appear on the screen).

Whichever method you use to calculate the timings, you can alter this for individual slides by using the **Slide Show** menu, followed by **Slide Transition**.

Setting up the show

Pull down the **Slide Show** menu and choose **Set Up Show**, select the options shown below (**Browsed at a kiosk** and **Using timings**)

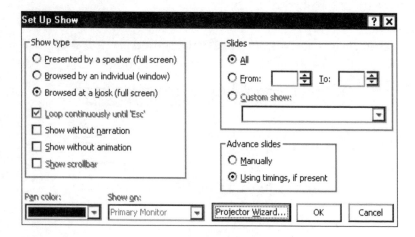

Note the button **Projector Wizard**; this is a feature that sets up the projector you are using.

Setting the timings automatically

Using the **Slide Show** menu and choosing **Slide Transition**, set the **Advance** box to the time you want to allocate to each slide (see the illustration) and click the **Apply to All** button.

Alternatively you can set individual times for each slide by using the **Apply** button.

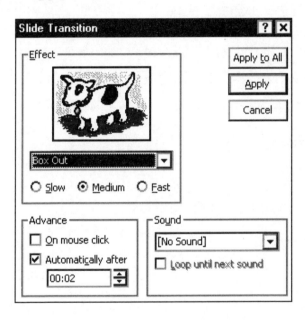

When you run your slide show, it will display automatically and continue forever (or until you stop it by pressing the **ESC** key).

Setting the timings manually

Pull down the **Slide Show** menu and select **Rehearse Timings**.

This will begin your slide show and you will see a timing box on the screen. This calculates the time it takes to advance each slide (you work through the show, using the mouse to advance the slides and the timer keeps a record of how long each slide takes).

At the end, you will be asked if you want to retain these timings and they will then be used to automate the show.

Printing

To print your file, click on the **Print** button on the upper toolbar.

If you pull down the **File** menu and select **Print** you will see the following dialog box that offers you various choices.

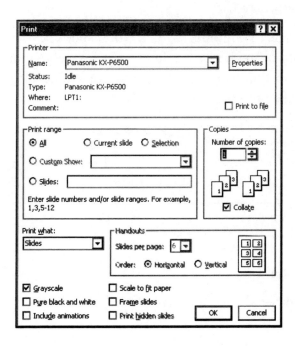

Print what

Slides

One to a page.

Handouts

If you select **Handouts** (2, 3, 4, 6 or 9 slides per page), you can print off audience handouts, which give your audience both something to take away and something to annotate during the presentation.

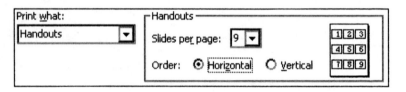

Notes pages

The slides and your notes are printed for each slide.

Outline View

Prints the outline view.

Options

There are several printing options in the (bottom of) the dialog box

Grayscale

Converts colours into shades of grey.

Pure black & white

This makes all colour fills into B&W and borders all unbordered objects.

Include animations

Includes any animations as part of the printout.

Scale to fit paper

Alters the scale to fit the paper size being used.

Frame slides

This prints a frame around each slide.

Print hidden slides

You can hide slides within your presentation and only show them if you wish, selecting this option would include them in the printout.

Saving Your Work

You should get into the habit of saving your work regularly so that any problems, whether hardware or software, do not cause too much loss of time or other problems.

To save your work you can click on the **Save** button on the toolbar along the top of the screen.

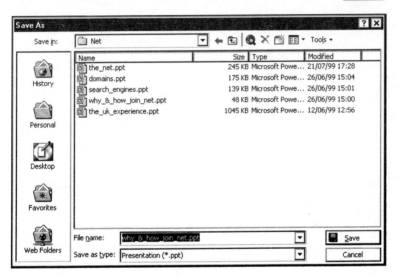

At this point, you can change where you save the file by clicking on the arrow to the right of **Save in** and alter the folder or disc you are saving to (use the buttons to locate the folder).

Next time you use the **Save** button to save your work the process will be automatic and there will be no dialog box appearing.

> If you want to save to a different folder or filename then use **File** and **Save As**.

Note the **Save as type** option; you can save your file in a variety of different formats so that it can be opened in another program or a different version of the program.

Text

You will be looking at the various ways of entering and manipulating text within your presentation.

Entering Text

This is simple, click where prompted and begin typing.

When entering body text use the **return** key to move on to the next point, a new bullet will appear below the original.

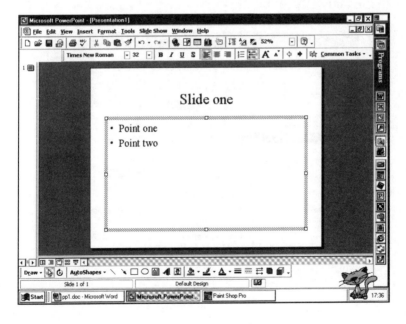

Altering the Font

Each design has fonts allocated to it, often these are ideal, but if you want to alter the fonts, there are several methods.

Highlight the text (by clicking and dragging the mouse to select the text), then click on the **Font** button along the upper toolbar and choose another font.

You can also alter the **Font Size** in the same way.

Alternatively, select the text and pull down the **Format** menu and select **Font**, this gives more choices.

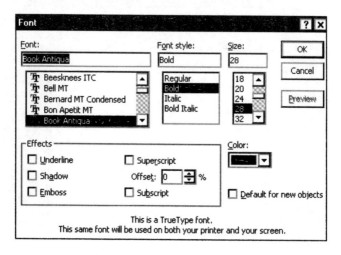

If you alter the **Master Slide**, the text within all the slides in the file changes to the new font/font size (see section on master slides).

Spell Checking Your Text

It is very easy to destroy your presentation by using incorrect spelling. Click the button along the upper toolbar and a dialog box will appear.

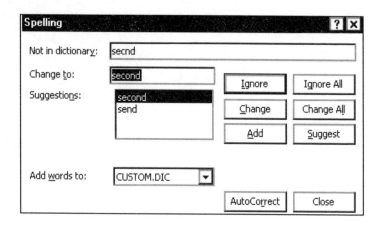

The way a spell checker operates is to compare every word you enter against a (finite) list of words.

If the word you type is not in the list, the spell checker program will identify it.

This does not mean it is wrong; merely that it is not in the dictionary.

You can **Add** words to your dictionary if you wish.

Graphics & Objects

It is useful and rewarding to add visuals to your presentation. You can add:

❖   ClipArt (from the library that comes with the program)

❖   Pictures or scanned images

❖   Graphs

❖   WordArt

❖   Tables

❖   Organisation Charts

❖   Other objects

ClipArt

Select the slide to which you want to add the image.

Click on the **Insert ClipArt** button on the **Drawing** toolbar (which should appear along the bottom of the screen, if it does not then pull down the **View** menu, select **Toolbars**, followed by **Drawing**).

The Microsoft Clip Gallery will appear.

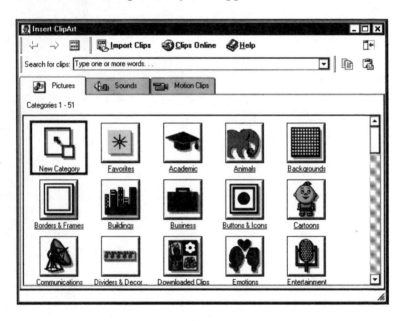

Select the category and then the image you want from the gallery and you will see it appear within the slide.

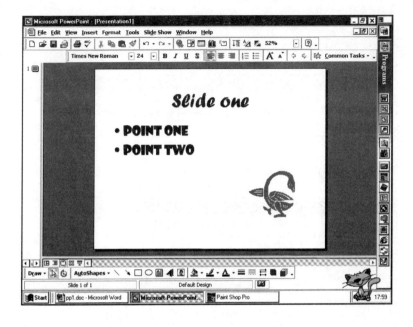

You can use the **Search** box by entering a word or phrase in the box and the program will find the appropriate images.

Here is a search on the word *cat*.

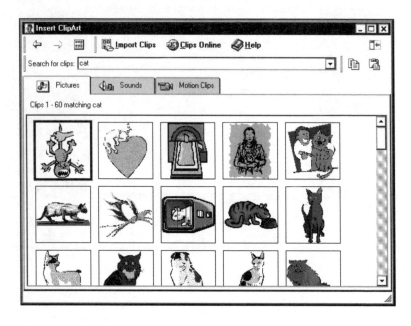

Pictures, sounds and videos

In a similar way to clip art, you can add (photograph quality) pictures, sounds and even motion (video) clips to your slide show.

You can use those installed in the **Clip Gallery** or you can insert others using the **Insert** menu.

Graphs

You can insert graphs by clicking on the toolbar button.

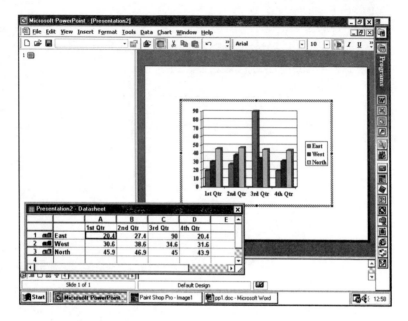

This is **Microsoft Graph** (an application that is accessed from all the main applications e.g. PowerPoint and Word).

You create your own graph by altering and/or adding to the data shown.

You will see some new buttons appear on the toolbar.

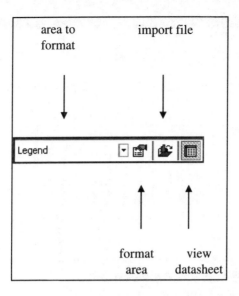

You alter the graph by using the various buttons and facilities. Graphs can be sized and so on in a similar way to other visuals.

Here is one I made earlier.

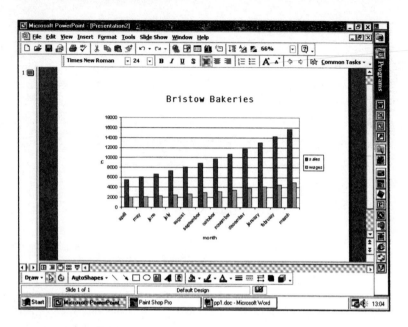

To alter a graph, double-click it and you can then edit it as you wish by using the various features of the **Graph** application.

You can insert data from a spreadsheet program such as Excel or insert an existing graph from Excel by using the **Insert** (**Object**) pull down menu (or **Paste** a graph from the originating program).

WordArt

Another type of object you can insert into your presentation is WordArt. You can create special text effects and fancy lettering for logos or titles by using this.

Click the **WordArt** button (upper toolbar) to begin the process; you will see the following screen.

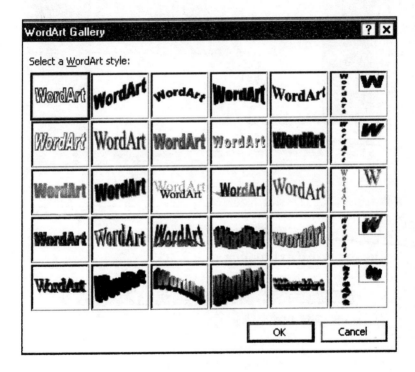

Select the style you want (you can change it later) and click **OK**, the screen will change to show a text entry box. Enter your text in the box (returning to create a new line) and then use the buttons to create the effect you want.

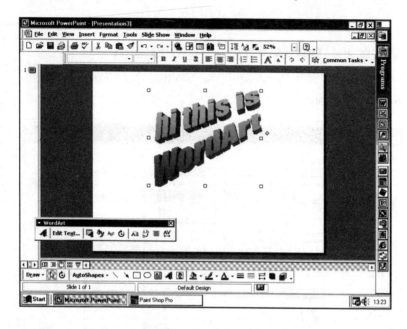

Your text will be displayed and you can then alter it by using the **WordArt** toolbar.

Once you have finished the text and effects, just click the mouse away from the object. To alter your WordArt object double-click it and WordArt will be loaded again.

Tables

Another useful design technique is tables.

Creating tables within PowerPoint

Insert a new slide, choosing the tables layout (as shown in the illustration).

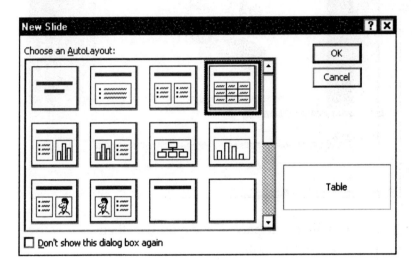

You will then see the following screen.

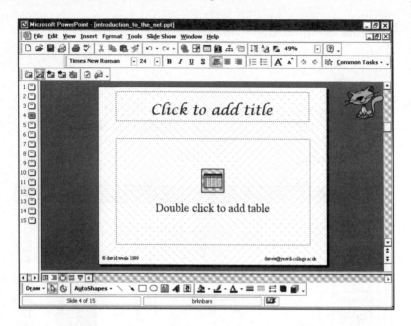

Double-click the image and decide how many rows and columns you want (you can add or delete them at a later stage if necessary).

An alternative to this is to pull down the **Insert** menu and select **Table**), this will insert a table into an existing slide (or you can click the **Table** button which lets you highlight the number of rows and columns you want in your table).

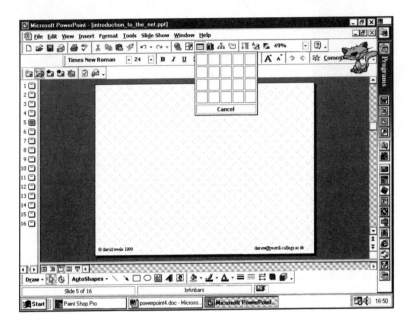

The table will appear, along with the tables toolbar (as shown in the illustration).

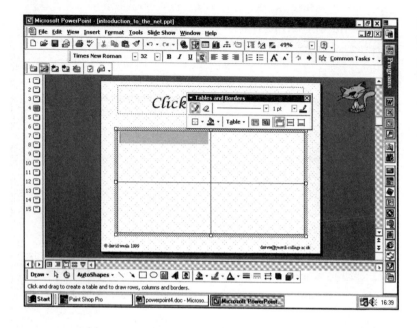

You can use the (table) buttons, in conjunction with the other toolbars to create the effects you want; here is an example.

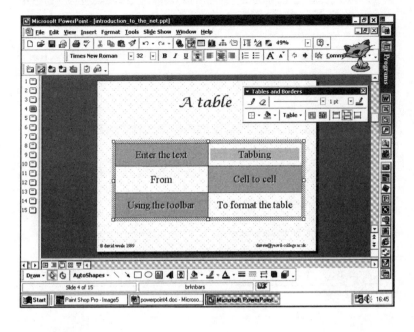

Word tables

Alternatively you can create a table using Word, to do so pull down the **Insert** menu and select **Picture**, followed by **Microsoft Word Table**.

The advantage is that you will be able to use the more extensive and sophisticated facilities available within Word. An example is shown below.

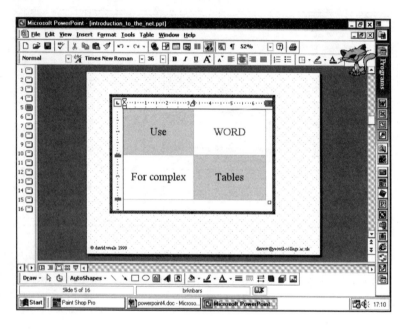

If you have an existing table, you can paste it into PowerPoint (and link it using **Paste Special** if you wish - linking means that if you alter the original in Word, the copy in PowerPoint will be updated automatically).

Organisation Charts

One of the advantages of a program such as PowerPoint is the variety of predesigned diagrams and other graphics available.

To insert an organisation chart into your presentation, use the organisation chart slide layout.

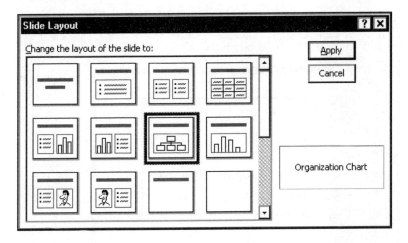

After selecting this, you will see the slide, double-click the symbol and you can begin to create your organisation chart.

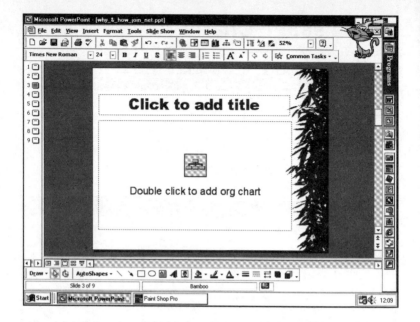

Alternatively, you can pull down the **Insert** menu and select **Object**, followed by **MS Organisation Chart 2**, or click the **Organisation Chart** button (if it is shown on your toolbar).

62

Whichever method you decide upon to begin the process, you will end up with the following screen.

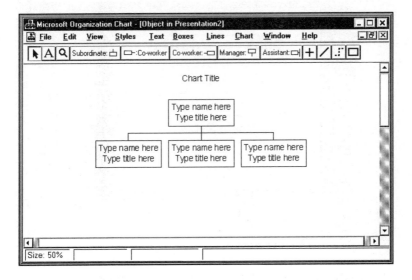

You enter the names and titles by highlighting the relevant text and overtyping and you can add or delete the boxes by using the various buttons and pull down menus.

Here is an example of a competed organisation chart.

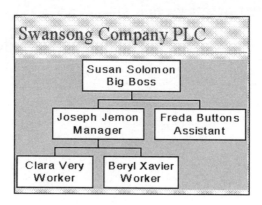

The commands specific to the organisation chart are described briefly below.

File Menu

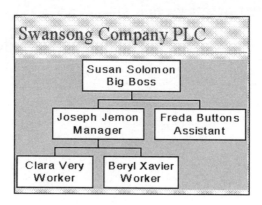

New	Ctrl+N
Open...	Ctrl+O
Close and Return to Presentation2	
Update Presentation2	
Save Copy As...	
Revert...	
Exit and Return to Presentation2	

Update Presentation

This updates the organisation chart in PowerPoint to be the same as the one you are working with in the Organisation Chart screen.

Revert

This discards any changes you have made since the last time you saved the chart.

Edit menu

Select and **Select Levels** enable you to select boxes within the chart.

You can also select all or part of the chart by clicking and dragging the mouse over the boxes you want to select.

View menu

You can size the chart and show the **Draw** tools, which can be very useful to add lines, etc., to an organisation chart.

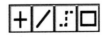

Styles menu

The menu show you a series of group styles which you can apply to any box(es) within your chart (that you have selected).

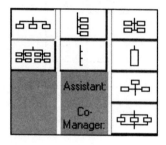

Text menu

Within this menu, you can alter the alignment, font or colour of selected text.

Boxes menu

Similarly, you can alter the look of selected boxes by altering the lines, borders, and colours, e.g. Border Style.

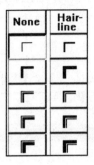

Lines menu

Here you can alter the line styles (thickness, colour, etc.) for selected lines.

Chart menu

This lets you change the Background Color.

Help menu

The organisation chart screen has its own specific help.

Other Objects

There are several other objects you can add to your presentation, e.g. **Microsoft Equation 3** (using this you can enter very complex mathematical symbols and equations).

To access these, pull down the **Insert** menu, followed by **Object** and select from the list.

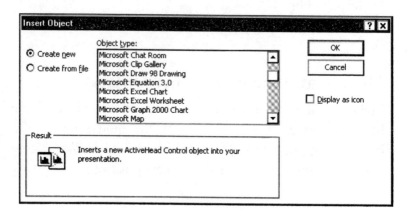

Artwork

Manipulating Images

There are various techniques that can be used to manipulate the image (and these can be applied to most visuals and objects).

Moving an Image (or Other Object)

Make sure that the image has been selected (it should have little squares around it) then click the mouse within the image (it becomes a four-headed cross) and *while holding down the mouse button* move to a new position.

Sizing an Image

There are two ways to achieve this.

Select the image and then position the mouse pointer on one of the small squares surrounding the image. The mouse pointer should become a small line with arrows at either end. While keeping the mouse button held down, move the mouse either in or out to resize the image.

Alternatively, click the image, pull down the **Format** menu, and select **Picture**, **Object** or **WordArt**. You will see a dialog box; all you need to do is to enter the percentage you want to scale to.

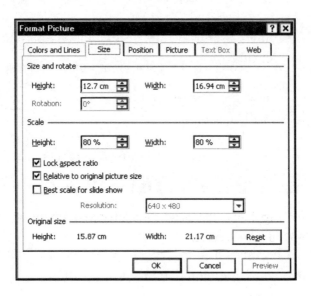

Alternatively, use the **Picture** toolbar buttons (if the toolbar is not displayed when you click the image, pull down the **View** menu and select **Toolbars**).

The **Format Picture** button will display the same dialog box shown above.

Cropping an Object

Cropping is different from sizing. Sizing makes the whole image smaller (or bigger), but when you crop an object, you remove part of the whole object.

This is sometimes useful to remove extraneous parts of a picture or other image.

To do this view the **Picture** toolbar and the cropping tool will be shown.

You then grab any corner or side of your object with the tool and remove part of the object.

You can bring back any part of a cropped image in the same way you removed it.

Here are two images, one before cropping and one after.

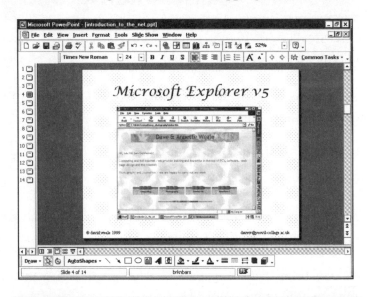

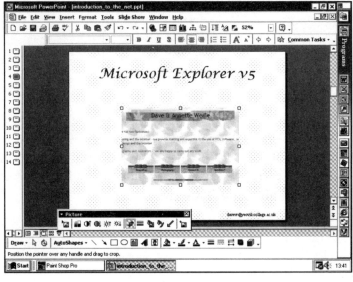

Customising Slides

This section deals with the methods of customising your presentation so that it stands out from other presentations.

The Master Slide

You can make changes to all the slides by amending the **Master** slide.

To do this, pull down the **View** menu and select **Master**. You choose which type of master to alter from the list shown below.

```
Slide Master
Title Master
Handout Master
Notes Master
```

You will then see the **Master** appear and any changes or additions you make to this will be reflected in all the slides of **that** style (i.e. if you have changed the **Slide Master** this will **not** affect the **Title** slide).

Below is an example of a **Slide Master** with the fonts changes and made larger. Any slides within that file will take on these new attributes.

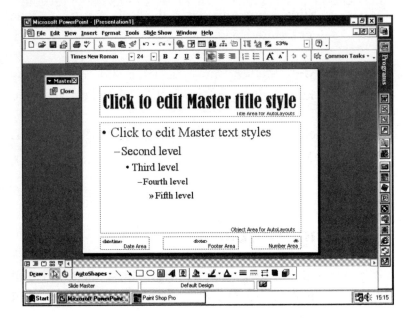

Deleting Slides

There are two ways to achieve this:

❖   In **Slide View** pull down the **Edit** menu and then select **Delete Slide**.

❖   In **Slide Sorter View** select the slide or slides by clicking on them and press the **Delete** key.

You can select multiple slides using the **Shift** or **CTRL** keys while you click the slides.

Drawing toolbar

If you are doing any work with graphics, then you will want to display the **Drawing** toolbar. I work with it permanently displayed.

To display any toolbar, pull down the **View** menu and select **Toolbars**. Click on your choice. The toolbar will be displayed.

There are some very useful tools here, for example you can add text boxes and arrows to any part of your slides and some need further investigation.

Draw

If you click on this, a further menu is displayed.

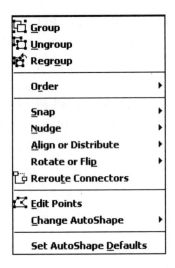

Grouping and Ungrouping

You may want to use only a part of an image or you may want to rearrange it. Ungrouping breaks up the image into its component parts.

It is not possible to ungroup certain types of image.

To ungroup an image, select it and then choose **Ungroup**.

A message *may* appear on the screen, which you can (if you want to ungroup the image) agree to.

You will see that the image is now made up of many sub-images all with little squares surrounding them.

Click outside the image and then click on any sub-image and you can move it, recolour it, size it or delete it as you wish (it may also be possible to ungroup a sub-image).

To select more than one component or object, hold down the **Shift** key while clicking the mouse on each item you want to select.

Merging images

You can join several images into one so that they form a single group, which can then be moved or resized, you can do this in several ways.

❖　　Hold down the mouse button and drag the mouse around the items. This will select all the items.

❖　　While holding down the **shift** key, click the mouse on each item you want to include within the group.

❖　　Pull down the **Edit** menu and choose **Select All**.

Then (whichever method is used) choose **Group** or **Regroup** from the **Draw** menu to combine all the images.

Superimposing One Image on Another

A useful technique is to use two or more images to create a new one.

Insert the two images and carry out any sizing or ungrouping you wish to.

Select one of the images and move it physically over the other and then select both and group them (so they form one image which can be manipulated).

Below is an example of two images used together, the original one was ungrouped, one part deleted and the components rearranged. The second image, the donkey, was sized and then moved onto the blackboard.

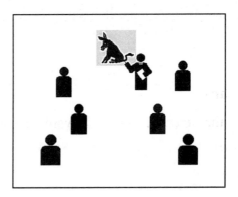

Order

If you place one object on top of another, the order in which these can be displayed can be critical to the result.

Think of the objects as being stacked, one on top of the next. The commands to vary the sequence are:

Bring to Front

This brings the selected object to the top of the pile.

Send to Back

This sends the selected object to the bottom of the pile.

Bring Forward

This brings the selected object forward one level in the pile.

Send Backward

This sends the selected object back one level in the pile.

Snap

There is an (invisible) grid and any object or text aligns itself to this. It makes lining up easier to achieve but does reduce fine control.

You can turn the **Snap to Grid** or **Snap to Shape** features on or off by selecting it (**Draw** and then **Snap**).

Nudge

If you have selected an object, you can nudge it in various directions.

Align or Distribute

This is used to align objects and/or text, you have to select more than one object or text for this to be usable, then simply pull down the **Draw** menu and **Align**. You have a choice of alignments and you can experiment with this technique.

Save the file before making any experimental changes to it.

Rotate or Flip

You can rotate or flip objects within PowerPoint. To do so, select the **Draw** menu and select **Rotate or Flip**. You will be given the following choices.

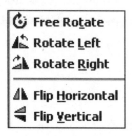

Free Rotate lets you grab any of the corners with the rotate tool and rotate to your heart's desire. Below is an example (the donkey has been flipped).

If your image will not allow you to choose **Rotate or Flip** then you may be able to **Ungroup** it (**Draw** menu) and then **Group** it again, it becomes a PowerPoint object and can be rotated.

Rotating Text

As well as being able to rotate objects, PowerPoint enables you to rotate text.

To do this simply select the text and use the **Drawing** toolbar, select **Draw** and then **Rotate or Flip**.

Edit Points

If you have created a freeform shape (e.g. by using any of the freeform tools (shown opposite) in the **AutoShapes Lines**), you can then move or edit the points within that object.

Change AutoShape

If you have created an AutoShape, and you select this option (while the AutoShape object is still selected) then you can choose another shape and the original shape will be converted into the new one.

AutoShapes

The AutoShapes menu is shown below.

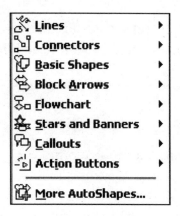

Each of these displays AutoShapes. The Flowchart shapes are shown for reference.

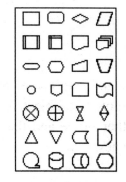

You select the symbol you want and then click and drag to produce the shape.

Once you have done this, you can manipulate the image as you wish, e.g. alter the shape, the colour and so on.

It is possible to create useful and interesting graphic shapes using this feature to produce the shapes and the adding colours and text as desired.

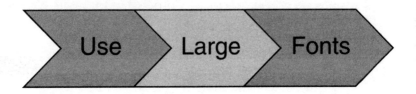

PowerPoint and the Web

With the growing importance and use of the Internet, the Microsoft Office programs are increasingly containing web tools.

These tools enable files to be converted into a format that can be used on the Internet and company Intranets without very much work or the need for extensive knowledge of HTML.

Web pages

Saving the pages as HTML

The simplest method is to save your file as a web page. To do so pull down the **File** menu and select **Save as Web Page**.

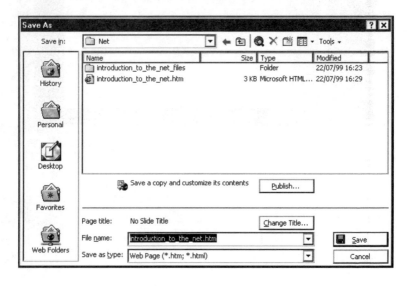

This saves the existing file as a web page (with a .HTM extension) and if you load it onto the Internet or your internal Intranet you will see a screen similar to this.

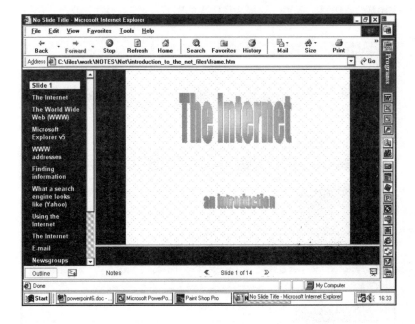

You can click the slide names (on the left of the screen) to see each individual slide or if you click the **Show** button on the right, the slide show will display.

Publishing your pages

Alternatively, you can click the **Publish** button, which allows you to select certain options

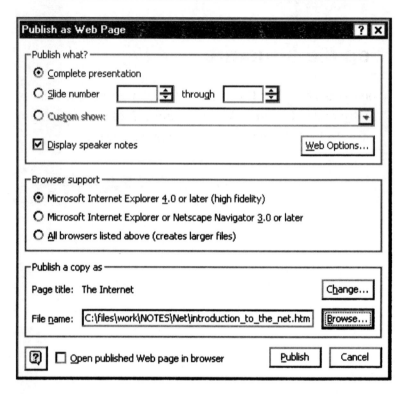

When you want to publish the pages to your web server then you need to enter the address for this in the **File name** section.

Note the option at the bottom, if you tick this then the browser will be loaded and the pages displayed without any further intervention on your part.

You can also see how your pages will look (as web pages) by using the **File** menu and then **Web Page Preview**.

Web file structure

When you save your PowerPoint file as web pages, what is actually created is an index page and a folder containing a file for each of the pages within the presentation.

Adding hyperlinks

You can add a hyperlink to a slide, either as an action button (explained later) or as a normal hyperlink.

To do this, click the **Hyperlink** button on the toolbar and enter the necessary data into the resulting dialog box. You will then be able to click the hyperlink and go to the file or web page identified in the link.

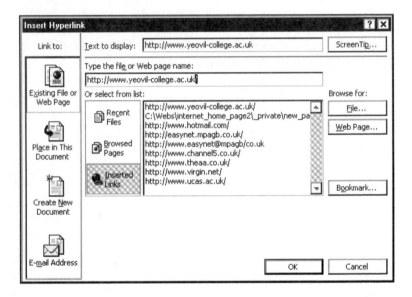

The Pull Down Menus

In this section of the book, I have covered the commands within the pull down menus *that have not been dealt with previously.*

You may see an arrow at the bottom of the pull down menus; this means that there are additional commands, which you can access by clicking the arrow.

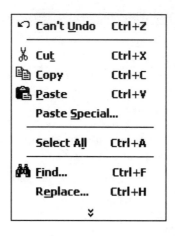

You can also set the full menus to (always) appear by using the **Tools** menu, followed by **Customize** and **Options**.

File menu

☐	<u>N</u>ew...	Ctrl+N
🖿	<u>O</u>pen...	Ctrl+O
	<u>C</u>lose	
🖫	<u>S</u>ave	Ctrl+S
	Save <u>A</u>s...	
🖳	Save as Web Pa<u>g</u>e...	
	Pac<u>k</u> and Go...	
	We<u>b</u> Page Preview	
	Page Set<u>u</u>p...	
🖶	<u>P</u>rint...	Ctrl+P
	Sen<u>d</u> To	▶
	Proper<u>t</u>ies	
	<u>1</u> \...\introduction_to_the_net.ppt	
	<u>2</u> \files\Slide one.ppt	
	<u>3</u> \...\why_&_how_join_net.ppt	
	<u>4</u> \...\NOTES\Net\domains.ppt	
	E<u>x</u>it	

Pack and Go

You can save a presentation on a floppy disc so that it can be used on any computer whether it has PowerPoint installed or not.

If you have used fonts in your presentation that may not be present on the host computer then you can embed them into the presentation.

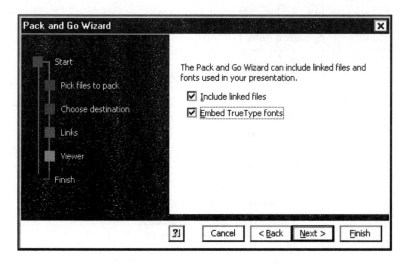

You can incorporate the viewer if the host computer does not have a copy installed.

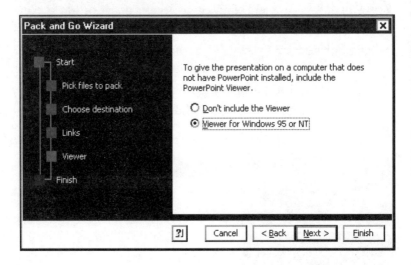

You will be prompted for additional discs if the files do not fit onto a single disc.

Send To

You can send a file to various places.

```
┌──────────────────────────────────────────┐
│  🖃 Mail Recipient                         │
│  🖃 Mail Recipient (as Attachment)...      │
│  📋 Routing Recipient...                   │
│  🗐 Exchange Folder...                     │
│     Online Meeting Participant             │
│  ──────────────────────────────────────   │
│  📑 Microsoft Word...                      │
└──────────────────────────────────────────┘
```

Mail Recipient

You can send the file via e-mail.

If your presentation consists of more than one slide, you will be given this choice.

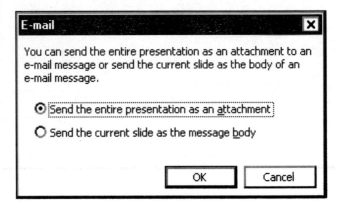

The e-mail program is then loaded and the file automatically included as an attachment or as part of the body of the message.

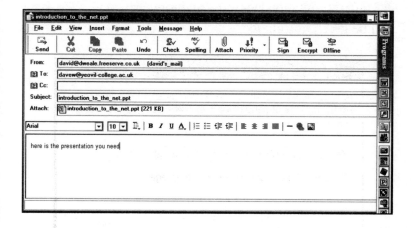

Routing Recipient

If you want the recipients to look at your file one at a time and (perhaps) add comments, then you can route the presentation to one recipient after another and each will see the previous comments. You can track the progress of the file and when it has been to all the recipients, it will automatically be returned to you.

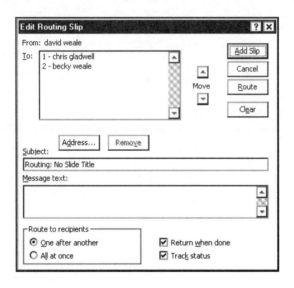

Exchange Folder

You can post the file to a Microsoft Exchange public folder, so that anyone with access to the folder can look at the file.

Microsoft Word

You can send the file to **Word**. You will see a dialog box, which gives you various choices about how the slides will appear within the Word document.

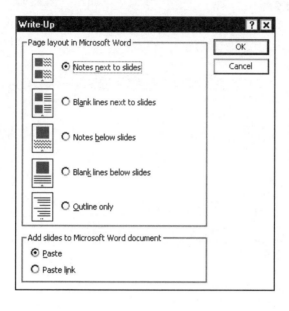

The results look like this.

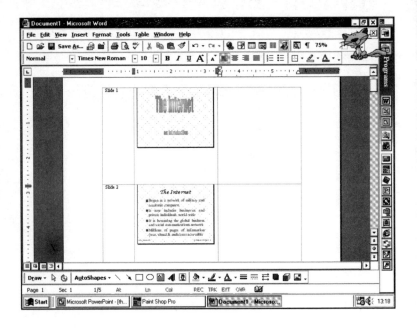

Properties

This displays screens of information about the file (some of which can be altered). The **Statistics** screen is shown for reference.

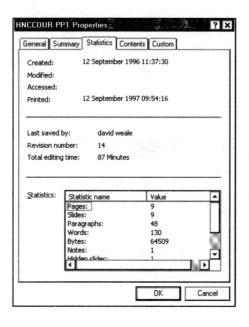

Edit menu

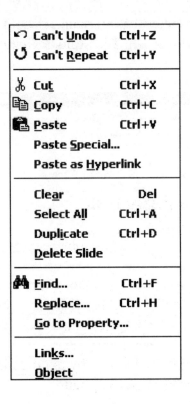

Cut, Copy and Paste

Remember that you can **Cut, Copy or Paste,** text or images using the appropriate buttons on the toolbar.

Paste Special

This is similar to the Paste command but gives you more control and allows you to create a link to the original application.

If an object is linked, it will be automatically updated when the original is changed.

Paste as Hyperlink

You can copy and paste text or objects as hyperlinks.

For example, you may want to paste a slide title as a hyperlink to that slide, so that if the viewer clicks on the hyperlink then they will jump to that slide.

You can also link to web sites by highlighting the link and clicking the **Insert Hyperlink** button.

Clear

Selecting this will clear (delete) the selected object or highlighted text.

Select All

This selects all the items (text & objects) on a particular slide **or** if in **Slide Sorter View** will select all the slides.

Duplicate

This allows you to duplicate a slide so that an identical copy is added to the presentation (next to the original). It only works in **Slide Sorter View**; select the required slide and then pull down the **Edit** menu and click on **Duplicate**.

Delete Slide

By pulling down the **Edit** menu and choosing **Delete Slide**, you can delete the current slide (or the selected slide(s) in **Slide Sorter View**).

You can also delete a slide in **Slide Sorter View** by selecting the slide(s) and then pressing the **Del** key.

You can use the **Undo** button if you quickly realise you have deleted the slide(s) accidentally.

Find

A standard text tool, this enables you to find words or parts of words within your presentation. The dialog box is shown below.

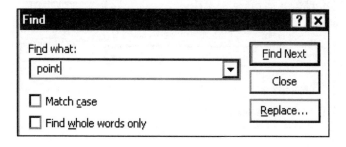

You enter the word or phrase you are looking for and click on the **Match case** and/or **Find whole words only,** if this is what you wish.

Click on the **Find Next** button and the first occurrence of the word will be found and then you can move to the next by clicking on the **Find Next** button and so on.

You can use **Shift** and **F4** to repeat the search.

Replace

Very similar to **Find** except you choose to replace the word or phrase with another.

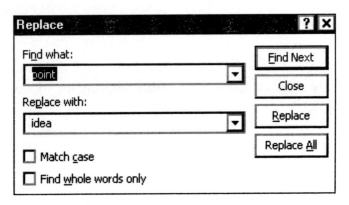

Go to Property

If you set custom properties (**File**, **Properties**) then you can go to the property within the slide using this option.

Links

If you select this option, you will see a dialog box displayed that lets you alter the links.

This option is not available until you have selected a linked object within your presentation.

Objects

You can edit objects by using the **Edit** menu followed by **Objects** or more quickly by **double clicking** the mouse on the object.

View menu

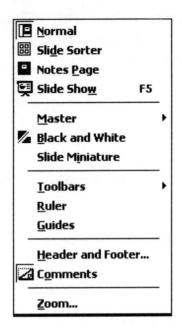

Black and White

You can display the slides in black and white.

Slide Miniature

This displays a small (colour) version of the slide in the top right-hand corner of the screen (but is only available if you have selected **Black and White**).

Toolbars

You can add or remove any of a number of different toolbars to your screen.

To do this, pull down the **View** menu and select **Toolbars**. You will see the dialog box shown below.

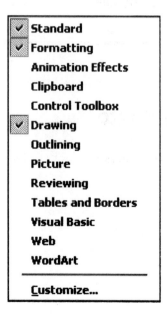

By selecting or deselecting the different toolbars you can add (or remove) them.

You can move a toolbar on the screen by clicking at its beginning (the cursor becomes a headed cross) you can then move it around the screen to a new position.

Once a toolbar is selected, you can change the shape by moving the mouse pointer along an edge until it becomes a two-headed arrow that can then be dragged to produce a new shape.

Rulers

You can display the vertical and horizontal rulers by selecting this option.

Guides

You can display or hide the guides by using the **View** menu and then **Guides**.

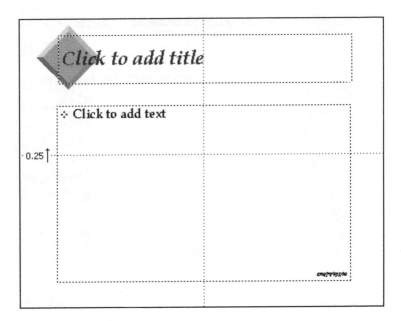

Guides are useful to position objects or text and they can be moved horizontally or vertically by clicking the mouse pointer on the guide and dragging it.

Header and Footer

You can insert the date and time, slide numbers and footers (you type in the text you want) using this feature.

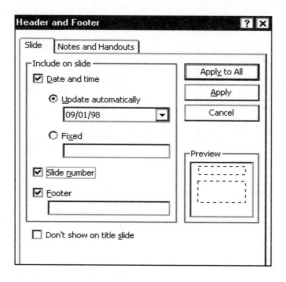

The **Notes and Handouts** option lets you do the same for the notes and handout pages.

You can see how footers appear from the illustration.

Comments

This displays the comments you have added to the slide (or hides the comments).

You need to have inserted the comments (**Insert** followed by **Comments**) as you can see in the upper left of the illustration.

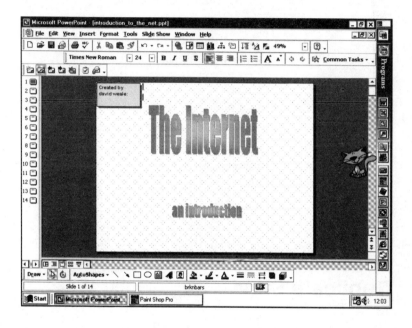

Insert menu

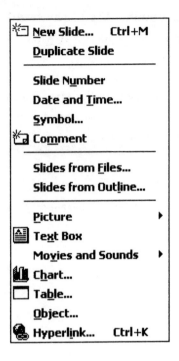

Duplicate Slide

This creates a copy of the current slide and inserts it into the slide show. Useful if you are making minor alterations to the slide.

Slide Number / Date and Time

Normally you would use the **Header and Footer** command (**View** menu) to insert page numbers and dates on the **Master** slide.

However, if you want to insert page numbers or dates on individual slides, you can use this feature. Remember you need to create a text box to do so.

Symbol

You can insert symbols from a variety of character sets into a text box.

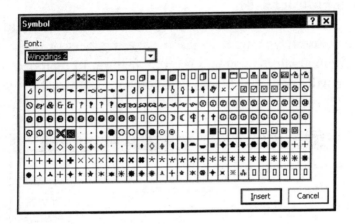

Comment

You can insert comments onto your slides; simply select this option and type in the comment you want to make. You can hide or display the comments by using the **View** menu and clicking **Comments**.

Slides from Files

This option lets you add slides from another file into your current presentation.

To do this, pull down the **Insert** menu and select **Slides from File**.

You will see a dialog box and you select which files you want to add.

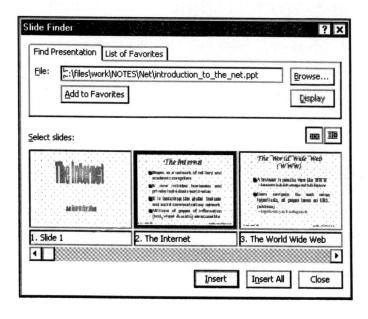

The new slides will be added after the current slide, and the other slides in the original presentation will be re-sequenced.

You may find it easiest to use **Slide Sorter View** and position the cursor where you want the new slides to be added.

Slides from Outline

This is slightly different in that PowerPoint will automatically create a slide show from an outline, using the outline levels as a guide, the first level text is treated as a heading and so on.

For example, if you created an outline within **Word** you could use this to create a PowerPoint presentation without having to retype the text. This works rather effectively and is a real time-saver.

You can see the results in the next illustration.

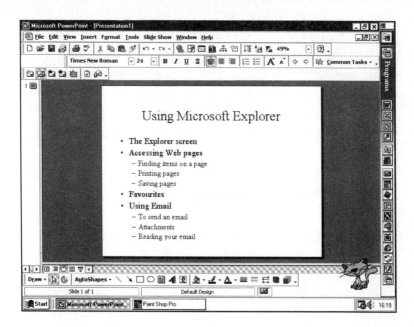

To do this, pull down the **Insert** menu and select **Slides from Outline**. Find the file you want to use and PowerPoint will convert it into a presentation. You will then need to make any alterations and to customise the presentation.

Pictures

These are treated in a very similar way to clipart; they can (mostly but not always, depending upon the type of file) be sized, recoloured, grouped and ungrouped and so on.

Scanned images require a large amount of disc space to store and tend to slow the system up when used.

A partial fix for this is to scale the scanned image before saving it so that it is the correct size.

However, you should not make it too small as increasing the size of an image can reduce the definition.

The type of file you save the image as will also affect the file size, some graphic formats create considerably smaller files (sometimes though with a loss of quality).

To insert a picture (that is not in the Microsoft Clip Gallery), pull down the **Insert** menu and select **Picture** and then **From File**.

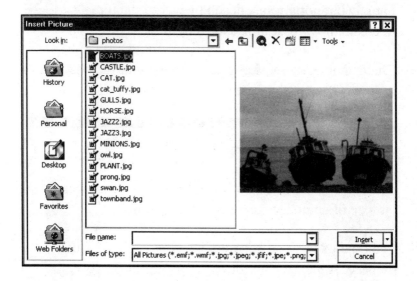

Find the picture on your hard disc and **Insert** it into your presentation.

Text Box

To create a textbox you click the **Text Box** button (**Drawing** toolbar) and then click and drag to create the box, adding text as desired.

The example below shows a text box (with the addition of a symbol) above the picture.

Movies and Sounds

Use this option to insert movie clips and sounds. You will
see a menu of choices (Gallery refers to the Clip Gallery).

<u>M</u>ovie from Gallery...
Movie from <u>F</u>ile...
<u>S</u>ound from Gallery...
Sou<u>n</u>d from File...
Play <u>C</u>D Audio Track...
<u>R</u>ecord Sound

If you choose to insert a movie from the gallery you can insert, play, add the clip to Favorites or find similar clips by using the buttons which appear when you click the movie clip you want (as you can see from the illustration).

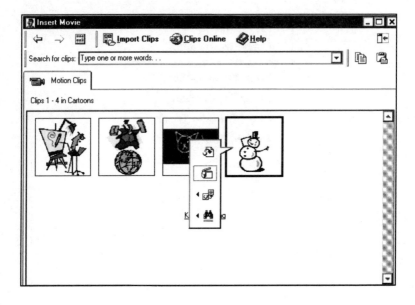

If you insert a movie then you will see an image that you can click to activate the movie when you view the slide show.

You can add sounds in a similar way.

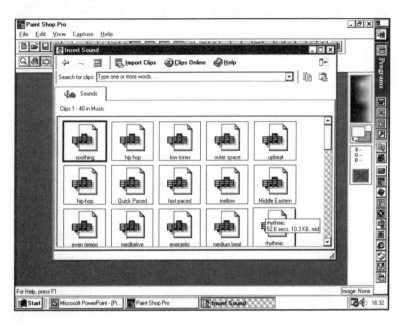

You will be asked whether you want the sound to play automatically or when clicked.

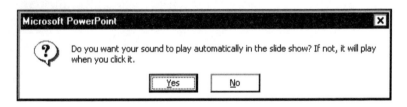

The final illustration shows both a movie clip and sound inserted into a slide, both of which play when you view the slideshow.

You can change the way in which movies and sounds are played by pulling down the **Slide Show** menu and selecting **Custom Animation**.

Format menu

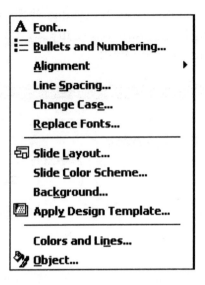

A <u>F</u>ont...

<u>B</u>ullets and Numbering...

<u>A</u>lignment   ▶

Line <u>S</u>pacing...

Change Cas<u>e</u>...

<u>R</u>eplace Fonts...

Slide <u>L</u>ayout...

Slide <u>C</u>olor Scheme...

Bac<u>k</u>ground...

Appl<u>y</u> Design Template...

<u>C</u>olors and Li<u>n</u>es...

<u>O</u>bject...

Font

You can alter the font by using the toolbar buttons, however you have more flexibility by pulling down the **Format** menu and then **Font**.

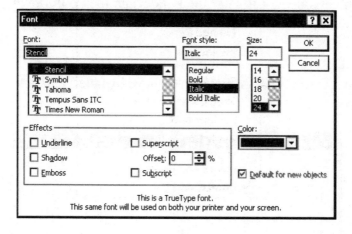

Bullets

If you want to alter the predefined bullets (again you can make these changes for an individual slide or for all the slides by altering the **Master Slide**), first select the text for which you want to alter the bullets and then pull down the **Format** menu and select **Bullets**.

There are various options. You can choose bullets from any character set or picture you have installed and you can alter the size.

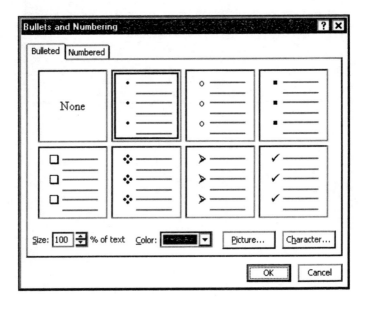

You can choose either a symbol from one of the character sets or a picture (illustrated below).

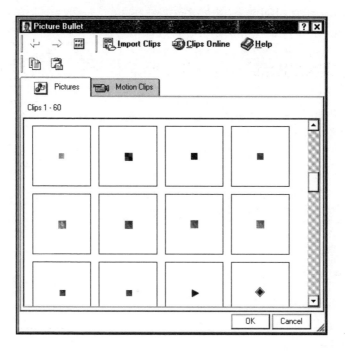

Alignment

To alter the alignment of paragraph(s), highlight the text and then either pull down the **Format** menu and select **Alignment** or use the alignment buttons on the toolbar. The Alignment menu gives more choice.

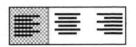

Alternatively, you can use the following keys (holding the first down while depressing the latter).

CTRL E	centre
CTRL J	justify
CTRL L	left
CTRL R	right

Line Spacing

Obviously hitting the **Return** key will create space; unfortunately it will also create another bullet. To avoid this, hold down the **Shift** key while depressing the **Return** key, this is a soft return and does not give rise to a new bullet.

However, this is a crude method and the most satisfactory method to alter the line spacing, whether for an individual slide or for the master slide is to use the **Format** menu and then **Line Spacing**.

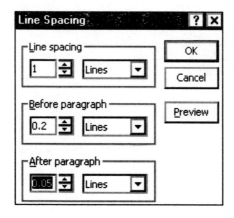

A dialog box will appear and you can alter the line spacing and the space before and after paragraphs as you wish.

Better still, you will be able to **Preview** the effect on screen as you make the changes.

Grab the dialog box and move it out of the way so that you can see the effect more clearly when you **Preview**.

You **must** highlight the text to alter the line spacing for more than one line (in this version of the program).

Change Case

You can change the case of the text you have typed in.

Believe me this is very useful, it is very easy to type text with the **Caps Lock** key on by mistake.

To use this feature you need to highlight the text and then pull down the **Format** menu and select **Change Case**.

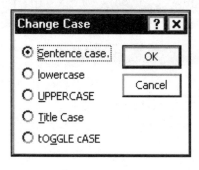

You can also use **Shift** and **F3** to alter the case of highlighted text.

Replacing Fonts

In the **Format** menu is an option called **Replace Fonts**.
This lets you alter one font to another, so that all type in
that font is changed to the new font.

The dialog box is shown below, you can use the arrows to
the right of each box to alter the choices.

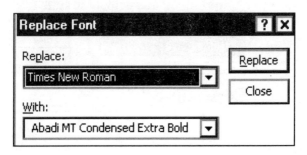

Slide Colour Scheme

You can change the standard colour scheme or click on **Custom** and alter the scheme as you wish.

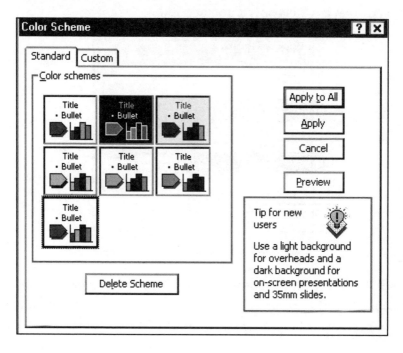

You can add any custom colour scheme you create to the standard schemes.

Background

Pull down the **Format** menu and select **Background**. You will see the following dialog box. Choose another colour and **Preview** or **Apply** it to your slides.

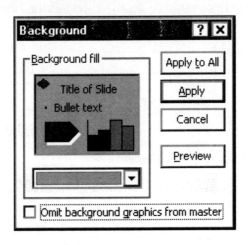

Be careful with the buttons **Apply To All** and **Apply**. Your choice will depend upon whether you want to change the background of all the slides or not.

Colour and Lines

You can add borders and fills to text boxes.

Click on the text box so that the boundaries are shown (you should see little squares positioned around the border).

Then pull down the **Format** menu and select **Colours & Lines**. Choose the colour and thickness of the line or fill and so on.

Alternatively, double-click the text box to display the same dialog box.

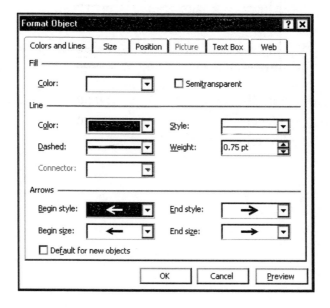

Object

Once you have selected an object or picture, you can alter the look of it by using the various tools within this dialog box (which is similar to the one illustrated above).

Format Painter

This button allows you to quickly alter how any text or object appears by copying the attributes (colour, shading, etc.) from one to the other (it may not work with graphs or pictures).

To work with the Format Painter, click on the text/object you want to copy the formatting from, then click on the Format Painter button and then drag the mouse pointer over the text/object you want to copy the attributes to.

Tools menu

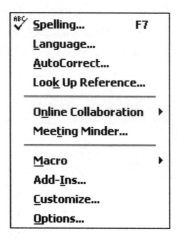

Language

You use this to set the language (for spelling and other checking purposes). The default is the choice of language you made when you installed Windows (to alter the default use the **Control Panel**).

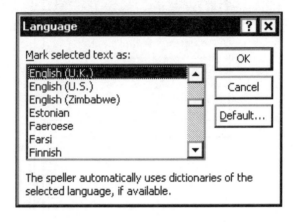

AutoCorrect

This sets various rules for the **AutoCorrect** feature. You can make any alterations you want, delete rules, add new rules, and create exceptions to the rules and so on.

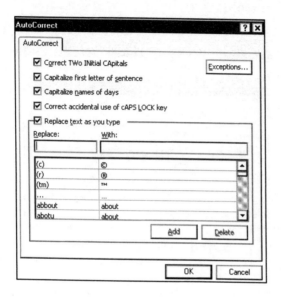

Look Up Reference

This lets you search certain (installed) reference tools. The reference is loaded automatically once you have clicked the **OK** button.

You can speed the search process by choosing how you want to search and what words you want to search for.

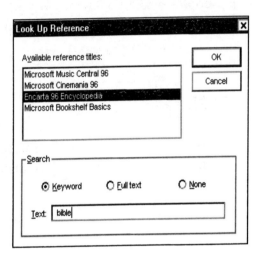

Online Collaboration

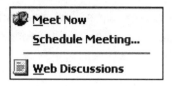

This enables you to set up online meetings through a server and to allow people to add comments to your work (this feature is available across all the Office 2000 applications).

Meeting Minder

This enables you to set up and organise meetings. It requires **Outlook** to be installed in order to function.

Macro

A macro (in its simplest form) is a series of commands, keystrokes and other activities. You record this series and you can then play it back without having to enter the keystrokes individually.

Add-Ins

These are additional programs, which enhance the use of PowerPoint. You can obtain add-in programs from a variety of sources, e.g. Microsoft's web site.

Customise

This enables you to add and delete buttons to reflect the way you personally work. After pulling down the **Tools** menu, select **Customise** and you will see a dialog box.

You can select from the different toolbars shown.

Add buttons (for that toolbar) by selecting the **Commands** tab and then grabbing the button and dragging it to **any** toolbar on the screen.

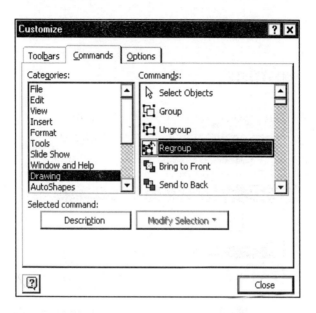

To remove a button, simply drag it off the toolbar.

If you decide that you have made a mess of any toolbar then the **Reset** button on the **Toolbar** menu lets you put everything back to its default position.

Options

In addition, in the **Tools** menu is **Options**. This is where you can make various changes to the way the program works.

Each of the tabs (**View**, **General**, **Edit**, etc.) contains program settings that you can alter from the default. Some are explained below.

Replace Straight Quotes with Smart Quotes

Replaces ordinary quotes (straight quotes) with curly ones, which you may prefer.

When selecting, automatically select entire word

When you use the mouse to select text, the text is highlighted in (groups of) words, if this feature is turned off then you will be able to select individual characters.

Use Smart Cut and Paste

Makes a space between words when the Clipboard contents are pasted into your slides.

Slide Show Menu

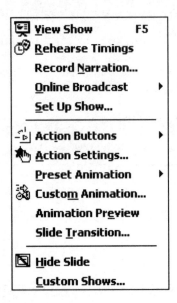

View Show

This runs the slide show; you can use the
Slide Show button instead.

Rehearse Timings

This runs the slide show, rehearsing the timings you have set **or** you can set timings using this option.

To set timings using the **Rehearse Timings** option, simply use the dialog box (shown below).

You can use the arrow symbol to advance the slides and the **Repeat** and **Pause** buttons as appropriate. When you have finished, you will be asked if you want to save the new timings.

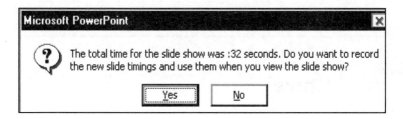

Record Narration

If you have the necessary sound card and microphone then you can add a spoken commentary to your slide show. This can be done while you are doing the presentation (with audience participation if you wish) or at some other time.

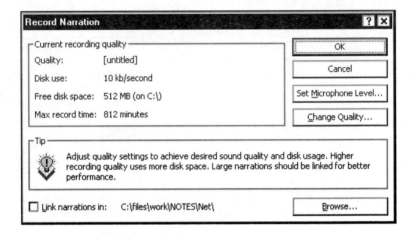

Online broadcast

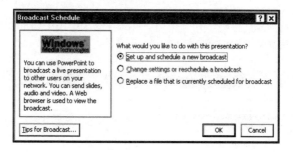

This enables you to broadcast a live presentation across a network.

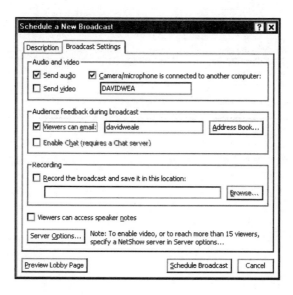

Set Up Show

This option gives you various choices on how you want to run the show.

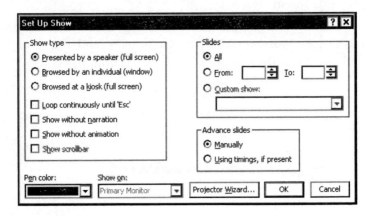

Action Buttons

You can add buttons to your slides, which are activated either by clicking the mouse on them or by moving the mouse over them.

You choose your button from the display and then click and drag the mouse to create the button within the slide.

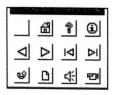

Then you enter the necessary data in the dialog box that will (automatically) appear.

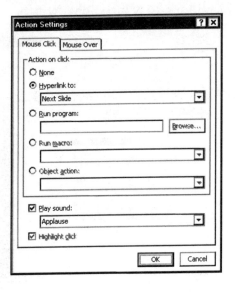

The following illustration shows an action button set to play the sound of applause, so whenever I click on the symbol, there will be the sound of applause.

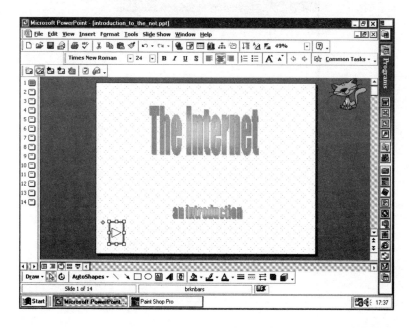

Another use of action buttons is to jump to a **Custom Show** or to another slide show by entering a **Hyperlink to**. This is simply the address of the slide show you want to include (either on the hard disc or on an Intranet or the Internet).

The arrow to the right of the **Hyperlink to** box will give you a choice of places you can jump to.

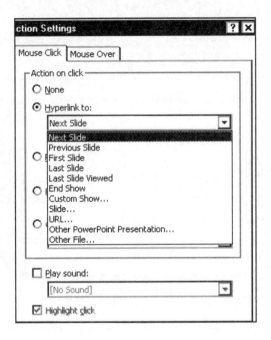

Your choice will determine the next step, for example, if you select **Other PowerPoint Presentation** then a dialog box appears enabling you to select the presentation you want to jump to.

Action Settings

This only becomes available when you have created an action button with settings. You can then alter the settings after selecting the button.

Preset Animation

This gives you a choice of animations (builds) to apply to your slide show. Animations are special effects that can be applied to text, graphics, buttons, etc. When you run your slide show you will see the animation take place.

✓	O<u>f</u>f
	<u>D</u>rive-In
	<u>F</u>lying
	<u>C</u>amera
	Flas<u>h</u> Once
	<u>L</u>aser Text
	<u>T</u>ypewriter
	<u>R</u>everse Order
	Drop-<u>I</u>n
	Fl<u>y</u> From Top
	A<u>n</u>imate Chart
	<u>W</u>ipe Right
	Dissol<u>v</u>e
	<u>S</u>plit Vertical Out
	<u>A</u>ppear

If you view the slides in **Slide Sorter View** then you can apply the animation to **all** the contents of all the slides by selecting all the slides (**Edit, Select All**). Alternatively, you can apply the animation to selected slides.

If you view the slides normally, you can select and apply animations to different elements of that slide e.g. the text.

Be warned, too many different animations can lead to the viewer paying more attention to the technique and not enough attention to your message.

Custom Animation

This gives you more control over the animations. You can select which parts of the slide to animate, in what order the animations take place, whether the animation is automatic or on a mouse click.

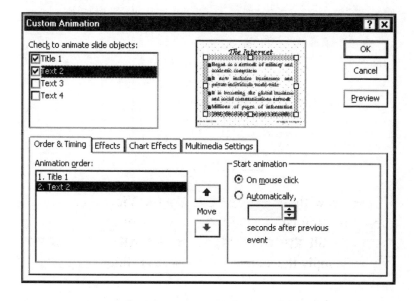

You can also change the **Effects** (the type of animation).

163

One of the professional effects you can use is to alter the colour of each line of text after it has appeared (as the next line appears) by choosing a colour in the **After animation** section.

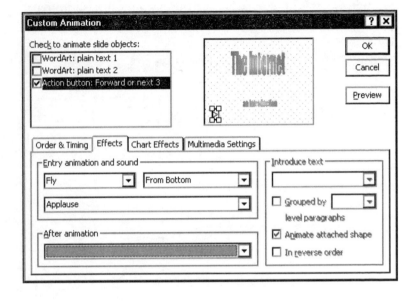

Animation Preview

This previews the animations you have set with a small preview display in the top right corner of the screen.

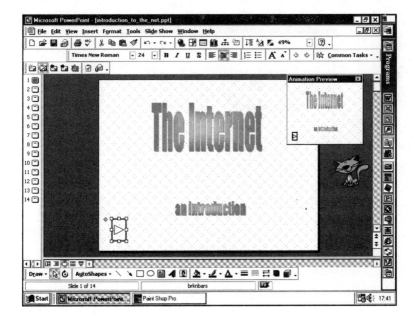

Slide Transition

This is a special effect between each slide, to set this select the **Slide Show** menu and then **Slide Transition**.

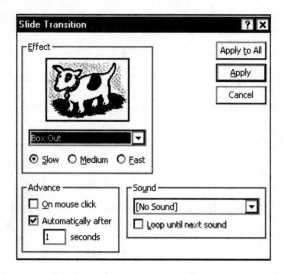

Select the transition from the (pull down) list and alter the options as you wish. You will see the effect reproduced as you make the changes.

Hide Slide

You can hide slides (within a presentation file) so that they do not display. This may be useful for certain audiences.

You can hide the current slide or if you are in **Slide Sorter View,** you can select several slides.

Remember that if you want to select several slides hold down the **Shift** key while clicking the mouse pointer on each.

To hide a slide use the **Tools** menu and then **Hide Slide**, or if you are in **Slide Sorter View** you can use the **Hide Slide** button (on the upper toolbar).

Displaying Hidden Slides

Type the character H while displaying the previous slide.

Custom Shows

You can build up slide shows that contain (some of the) slides from the original slide show.

You may want to do this because you are dealing with a variety of audiences, which require a different version of the original.

Click on **New** and then you will see the following dialog box.

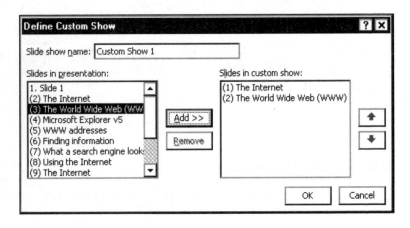

Help menu

```
┌─────────────────────────────────────┐
│ ?  Microsoft PowerPoint Help    F1   │
│    Hide the Office Assistant         │
├─────────────────────────────────────┤
│ ?  What's This?          Shift+F1    │
│    Office on the Web                 │
├─────────────────────────────────────┤
│    Detect and Repair...              │
├─────────────────────────────────────┤
│    About Microsoft PowerPoint        │
└─────────────────────────────────────┘
```

The Office Assistant

The assistant is normally always on screen or can be called from the menu by selecting **Microsoft PowerPoint Help**.

My assistant is a cat; yours can be any of the various figures in the gallery (to alter your assistant, click the right-hand mouse on your present assistant and **Choose Assistant**).

To get help double-click your assistant and you will see a dialog box where you ask your question.

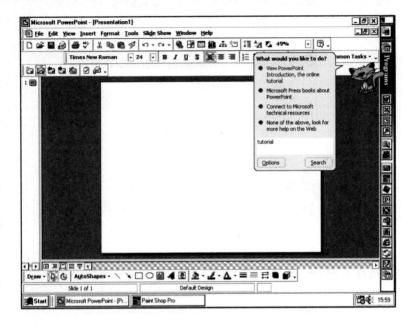

The Options Button

You can choose a new assistant by clicking the **Gallery** tab.

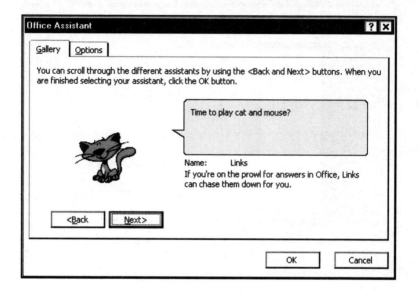

Alternatively if you select the **Options** tab, you can make various changes to the assistant.

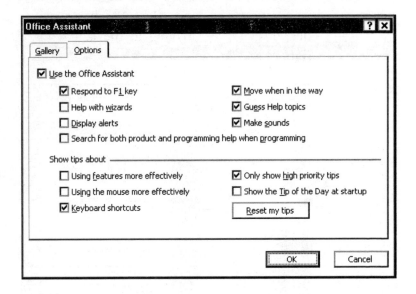

The Search Button

You type in a query and click the **Search** button. The results will be displayed; you then select which answer is closest and click this, finally arriving at the actual help screen on the right of the screen.

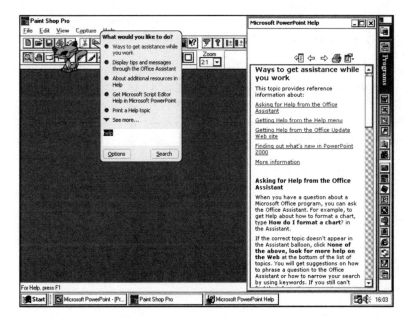

You can move around the help screens by clicking the hyperlinks (which are underlined and normally in blue).

Note the buttons along the top of the help screen; the first of these is the **Show** button used to display the more traditional method of obtaining help.

The other buttons enable you to move back or forward through the screens you have looked at or to print out the text. There is an options button on the far right which adds certain features.

Using the Show button

As you can see from the illustration, you have the **Contents**, **Answer Wizard** and **Index** options.

Contents

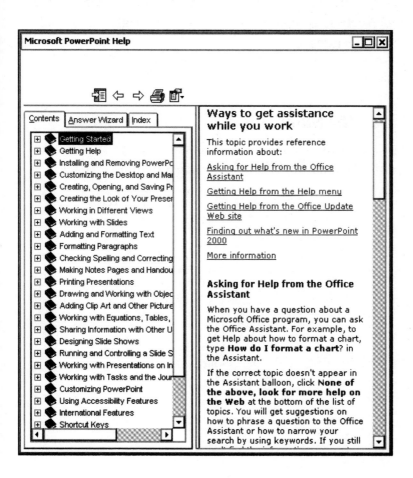

As you can see from the picture, the contents are like a series of books or chapters on the various aspects of the program.

Each book can be opened by double-clicking on it to reveal the sections within that book.

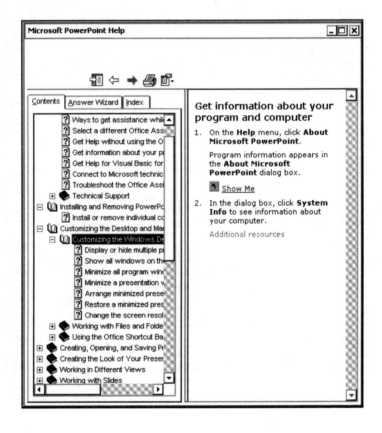

Answer Wizard

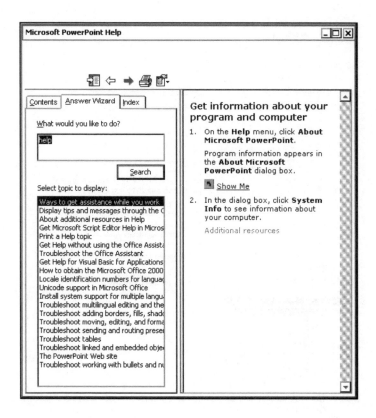

Instead of choosing from a list, here you type in the word or phrase and the nearest equivalents are displayed so you can select the one you want. The details are then shown in the right pane.

Index

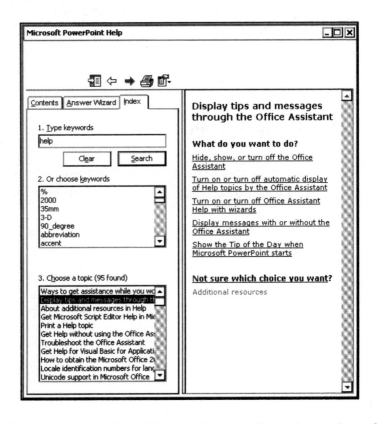

This includes a list of keywords as well as the option of typing a keyword.

What's This?

Clicking on this displays a tool. You drag this over the problem area and click to see an explanation of the topic.

Office on the Web

This option will connect you to the Microsoft site on the Internet. Your browser (e.g. Microsoft Explorer) will be loaded and so will the site.

About Microsoft PowerPoint

This displays information about the program.

Coping with Presentations

First Things

❖ Decide **WHAT** you want to achieve.

❖ Do you want to impart information or to persuade your audience in some way (e.g. to change their beliefs or attitudes)?

❖ Decide on the type of audience you are addressing and consider what they want from the presentation. Pitch the level of your presentation carefully; audiences vary in their attention span, intellectual ability, etc.

❖ Decide upon the best way to get your message across for the specific audience you are presenting to.

The Material

Write down the main points and then underneath write the detail. **Outline View** is a very useful tool for this.

The audience likes to have something to take away, so prepare a handout or copy of the OHPs you have used.

The Presentation

Always introduce the material and yourself to the audience and remember to wrap it all up at the end by summarising what you have told them.

Your voice is of primary importance, keep it slow and interested, emphasise the important points and the changes of topic, this keeps your audience awake. Maintain eye contact with as many of the audience as possible. Always practise, preferably in front of a live audience or video camera.

The audience is most likely to have a worthwhile experience if you exude enthusiasm, seem to be enjoying yourself and appear to know your subject.

The Environment Itself

Always check the room, seating, lighting and the display equipment (computer, OHP, projector, etc.).

Make sure that all the audience can actually see the screen easily (try not to stand in front of it). Arrange the seating and adjust any other environmental features (heating, lighting, etc.) as necessary.

Using Software

Keep a consistent style throughout the slides. Use clipart, charts or drawings to make points or to amuse but be careful not to detract from the actual message.

Keep the slides as simple as possible, too much detail is pointless and counter-productive, the purpose of the slides is to emphasise the main points of your talk not, usually, to replace the talk itself.

Make sure all the audience can read the slides (are the fonts large enough for those at the back of the room).

Slide Layout

Use initial capital letters but then lower case (i.e. not all capitals).

Keep the number of words, lines, numbers or graphic images to the absolute minimum for each slide (the maximum number of lines should ideally not be more than six).

Make sensible use of fonts and remember that you need to use large fonts so that the audience can read them easily without effort. It is likely that font sizes less than 18 points will not be readable, in many cases the larger the text the more effective it will be.

Creating a professional finish by ending with a blank coloured slide or a slide with your company logo. You can press the **B** character on the keyboard to blank the screen during presentations.

Use the **Rehearsal** feature to time your slide show (**Slide Show** and then **Rehearse Timings**).

Colours and Things

Be careful with your use of colour.

Try to avoid complicated images or backgrounds as these can be confusing to the audience and detract from the points you are trying to put across.

Be aware of contrasts, dark letters on a light backdrop show up well, charts and diagrams also look good with a light (but not too bright) background.

Index

N

O

P

Q

R

S